Data Structures and Algorithms:

Insights and Applications

By

Michael Andrew Lambert Jr

Abstract

This work provides a comprehensive exploration of searching and indexing algorithms within the realm of computer science, spanning nine chapters that delve into fundamental concepts, practical applications, and personal reflections. Chapter 1 introduces the importance of efficient data retrieval in the context of modern computing. Chapters 2 through 6 examine various searching techniques, including Jump Search, Binary Search, and advanced indexing methods such as hashing and tree-based structures. Key concepts such as the Zipf distribution are discussed in Chapter 7, highlighting their significance in natural language processing and data organization.

In Chapters 8 and 9, the narrative shifts to personal engagement with the material, reflecting on practical implementations and the learning journey. Insights gained from hands-on coding experiences, collaborative discussions, and the application of algorithms in real-world contexts underscore the importance of algorithmic efficiency in software development. The final chapter synthesizes key themes, emphasizing the critical role of searching and indexing in managing vast datasets and the implications for future software projects.

Overall, this work emphasizes the intersection of theoretical understanding and practical skills, preparing readers to navigate the complexities of data retrieval and management in their academic and professional endeavors.

Table of Contents

CH 1: Introduction to Searching and Indexing Algorithms **9**

CH 2: Fundamentals of Searching Algorithms **19**

CH 3: Advanced Searching Techniques **29**

CH 4: Hashing and Collision Resolution **43**

CH 5: Tree-Based Indexing **51**

CH 6: Real-World Applications of Searching Algorithms **61**

CH 7: Understanding the Zipf Distribution **71**

CH 8: Reflective Practices in Learning Algorithms **115**

CH 9: Summary and Key Takeaways **119**

Bibliography **125**

Chapter One

Introduction to Data Structures and Algorithms

Overview of Data Structures and Algorithms

This chapter introduces foundational concepts in data structures and algorithms, highlighting their significance in software engineering. The content emphasizes the critical relationship between data structures and algorithms, which is essential for effective problem-solving in computer science.

Key insights are drawn from Clifford A. Shaffer's "A Practical Introduction to Data Structures and Algorithm Analysis," particularly the initial chapters. These sections lay the groundwork for understanding the philosophical aspects of data structures and the pivotal role algorithms play in solving complex problems, alongside the necessary mathematical foundations, including sets, relations, logarithms, and recurrences.

Key Concepts Explored

Fundamental Definitions

A comprehensive understanding of data structures and algorithms requires precise definitions of key terms:

- **Type**: A classification that dictates the nature of a variable's value and the operations applicable to it, encompassing both simple types (e.g., integers, characters) and more complex classifications.
- **Data Item**: The smallest unit of meaningful data, representing an individual piece of information like a number or letter, showcasing the content a variable can hold.

- **Data Type**: A category defining a group of data items with similar properties and operations, affecting how data is stored and processed within a program.
- **Abstract Data Type (ADT)**: A conceptual model focusing on the operations on data rather than implementation details. ADTs aid in designing and utilizing data types, represented by structures such as stacks, queues, and lists.
- **Data Structure**: A method for organizing and storing data to enable efficient access and modification, encompassing the implementation of one or more ADTs. Common examples include arrays, linked lists, trees, and hash tables.
- **Class**: A blueprint in object-oriented programming that defines attributes (data members) and behaviors (member functions) for objects, encapsulating data structures and ADTs.

- **Member Function**: A function within a class that operates on objects instantiated from that class, interacting with the class's data members.
- **Data Members**: Variables declared within a class representing the properties of an object, storing unique data relevant to instances of that class.

Interrelationships Among Concepts

The interconnections among these definitions highlight the cohesive structure of data handling in programming. Types categorize data items, while ADTs provide a theoretical framework guiding the design of data structures. In object-oriented programming, classes unify these elements, encapsulating both data and behavior into a manageable format.

Mathematical Foundations

The chapter also covers essential mathematical concepts crucial for algorithm analysis. Topics such as logarithms, sets, and relations are explored to establish a basis for understanding algorithm efficiency and performance implications. Asymptotic analysis becomes a central focus, enabling assessment of algorithm performance relative to varying input sizes, a concept closely tied to Moore's Law.

Conclusion

This exploration establishes a robust foundation for further study in data structures and algorithms. By grasping fundamental concepts, interrelationships, and mathematical principles, individuals are well-prepared to delve into more advanced topics. The insights gained will be invaluable for future endeavors in software development, emphasizing structured problem-solving and performance optimization.

As the study continues, the ability to articulate complex technical concepts and analyze algorithm efficiency will become increasingly essential, laying the groundwork for successful application in real-world scenarios.

Chapter 2

Algorithm Analysis

Overview

This chapter delves into the critical field of algorithm analysis, emphasizing the importance of understanding algorithm efficiency through best, worst, and average case scenarios, as well as exploring asymptotic analysis. Key notations, including Big O, Big Omega, and Big Theta, provide a framework for articulating the running time of various algorithms accurately.

Key Concepts

Asymptotic Analysis

Asymptotic analysis serves as a framework for evaluating algorithm efficiency. It involves comparing the growth rates of functions to determine how the performance of an algorithm changes relative to the size of the input. This analysis is crucial for understanding how algorithms behave under different conditions.

Big O, Big Omega, and Big Theta Notation

These notations are central to algorithm analysis. Big O notation represents the upper bound of an algorithm's running time, indicating the worst-case scenario. Conversely, Big Omega describes the lower bound, or best-case scenario. Big Theta notation provides a tight bound, signifying that the algorithm's performance is asymptotically equal to both the upper and lower bounds. Mastering these notations equips individuals with the tools to analyze and communicate algorithm performance effectively.

Time Complexity

Determining time complexity through code snippet analysis is a significant focus. Recognizing patterns within loop structures, particularly nested loops, is essential, as these often lead to polynomial time complexities. For instance, in the provided nested loop example, the outer loop's execution influences the overall time complexity, leading to an $O(n^2)$ classification due to the quadratic growth associated with the sum of the first n-1 integers.

Insights and Reflections

Engaging in this analysis revealed the complexities of understanding performance characteristics. The abstract nature of asymptotic analysis posed challenges; however, breaking problems into smaller steps facilitated comprehension. The collaborative nature of the work fostered a rich exchange of ideas, enhancing the overall learning experience.

Surprises and Challenges

A fascinating realization was the nuanced comparison between exponential and polynomial time complexities. Understanding when one growth rate overtakes another, particularly through logarithmic analysis, highlighted the need for a strong mathematical foundation. This challenge necessitated revisiting logarithmic properties, reinforcing the connection between mathematics and computer science.

Skills and Knowledge Gained

This chapter not only enhanced algorithm analysis capabilities but also improved mathematical skills, particularly in logarithmic functions. The experience emphasized the significance of collaborative learning, where diverse viewpoints contributed to a deeper understanding of the material.

Application of Concepts

The knowledge acquired regarding asymptotic analysis and time complexity is directly applicable to software development projects. Understanding how to assess algorithm efficiency is essential for making informed design choices that prioritize performance and scalability. This foundational knowledge will serve as a guiding principle in future software engineering endeavors.

Conclusion

In summary, this exploration of algorithm analysis enriched understanding of key performance metrics in computer science. The concepts learned are foundational for advancing in algorithm design and optimization, preparing for future challenges in the field. As the study continues, the insights gained will undoubtedly inform approaches to developing efficient and scalable software solutions.

Chapter Three

Stack and Queue Data Structures

Stack Data Structure

A stack follows the Last-In-First-Out (LIFO) principle, meaning elements are added and removed from one end, known as the top. The primary operations associated with a stack include:

- **Push**: This operation adds an element to the top of the stack.
- **Pop**: This operation removes the element from the top of the stack (Shaffer, 2011).

Structure

Stacks can be implemented using either arrays or linked lists. They support operations primarily at the top of the structure.

Function

Stacks are particularly useful in scenarios that involve step-by-step processing, such as managing function calls in programming languages. They enable backtracking mechanisms, like undo operations in text editors (Barnett & Del Tongo, 2008).

Queue Data Structure

In contrast, a queue operates on the First-In-First-Out (FIFO) principle, where elements are added at the rear and removed from the front. The key operations in a queue are:

- **Enqueue**: This operation adds an element to the rear of the queue.
- **Dequeue**: This operation removes the element from the front of the queue (Shaffer, 2011).

Structure

Queues can also be implemented using arrays or linked lists and maintain the order of elements based on their arrival times.

Function

Queues are ideal for scenarios requiring sequential order processing, such as printing tasks. They facilitate buffering and synchronization tasks in operating systems (Barnett & Del Tongo, 2008).

Differences Between Stacks and Queues

Order of Operations

- **Stack**: Uses LIFO order, making it suitable for applications requiring depth-first search or recursive function calls (Shaffer, 2011).
- **Queue**: Uses FIFO order, suitable for handling tasks in the order they arrive, such as task scheduling or print queues (Barnett & Del Tongo, 2008).

Usage Scenarios

- **Stack**: Commonly used in situations where the last item added should be the first item removed, like managing function calls or undo operations.

- **Queue**: Employed when items must be processed in the order they are received, such as in task scheduling or print queues.

Implementation Considerations

- **Stack**: Efficient for operations at one end (the top), but may be inefficient for random access to elements (Shaffer, 2011).
- **Queue**: Efficient for operations at both ends (front and rear), ensuring that elements are added and removed in the correct order (Barnett & Del Tongo, 2008).

Overall, stacks and queues are essential data structures that serve different purposes depending on their ordering rules (LIFO for stacks and FIFO for queues) and their implementation (arrays vs. linked lists). Understanding how they function and their applications is crucial for selecting the appropriate data structure for specific programming needs.

Implementation Example: Stack Using Linked List

The following algorithm initializes an empty stack using a linked list, designed to track inspections in an automobile assembly line. It defines a Node class to represent each element in the stack and a Stack class with methods for pushing and popping elements. The push method adds a new inspection stage onto the stack, while the pop method removes the top element, simulating the completion of an inspection. The printAndPopAll method sequentially pops and prints each element, representing the process of inspecting a vehicle at each station in the assembly line. This implementation ensures efficient operations with constant time complexity O(1) for both push and pop operations.

Java Code Example

```java
class Node {
   int value;
   Node next;

   public Node(int value) {
      this.value = value;
   }
}
class Stack {
   private Node top;

   // Push method to add items to the stack
   public void push(int value) {
      Node newNode = new Node(value);
      newNode.next = top;
      top = newNode;
   }

   // Pop method to remove items from the stack
   public int pop() {
      if (top == null) {
         throw new IllegalStateException("Stack is empty");
      }
      int value = top.value;
      top = top.next;
      return value;
   }

   // Print stack elements as they are popped off
   public void printAndPopAll() {
      while (top != null) {
         System.out.println("Popped value: " + pop());
      }
   }
```

```java
public static void main(String[] args) {
    Stack stack = new Stack();
    stack.push(2);
    stack.push(1);
    stack.push(0);

    stack.printAndPopAll();
  }
}
```

Reflections on Learning

During this exploration of data structures, I engaged in discussions and hands-on activities that deepened my understanding of stacks and queues. Key learning points included:

- The distinctions between array-based and linked list implementations, particularly regarding memory allocation.
- The practical applications of stacks and queues in real-world scenarios, such as managing assembly line inspections.
- The significance of selecting the appropriate data structure to enhance performance.

Overall, this study of stacks and queues provided invaluable insights into efficient data handling and problem-solving in programming.

Chapter 4

Implementation of Binary Search Trees

In computer science, the Binary Search Tree (BST) serves as an essential data structure, allowing for efficient data organization and retrieval. A BST is characterized by its hierarchical structure, where each node can have a maximum of two children: a left child and a right child. The BST maintains a sorted order, facilitating efficient search, insertion, and deletion operations.

Node Class

The foundational component of a BST is the Node class. Each node contains an integer value and references to its left and right children, thus forming the building blocks of the tree.

```
class Node {
   int value;
   Node left, right;

   public Node(int item) {
      value = item;
      left = right = null;
   }
}
```

This structure allows for dynamic creation and linking of nodes, essential for the flexible nature of binary trees.

BinarySearchTree Class

The BinarySearchTree class manages various operations within the BST, such as insertion and search. The class begins with a root node initialized to null and includes methods for inserting new values and searching for existing ones.

```
public class BinarySearchTree {
   Node root;

   BinarySearchTree() {
      root = null;
   }

   void insert(int value) {
      root = insertRec(root, value);
   }
```

```
Node insertRec(Node root, int value) {
   if (root == null) {
      root = new Node(value);
      return root;
   }
   if (value < root.value) {
      root.left = insertRec(root.left, value);
   } else if (value > root.value) {
      root.right = insertRec(root.right, value);
   }
   return root;
}
boolean search(int value) {
   return searchRec(root, value) != null;
}

Node searchRec(Node root, int value) {
   if (root == null || root.value == value) {
      return root;
   }
   if (value < root.value) {
      return searchRec(root.left, value);
   }
   return searchRec(root.right, value);
}

void populateTree(int[] values) {
   for (int i = 0; i < values.length; i++) {
      insert(values[i]);
   }
  }
}
```

This implementation highlights the use of recursion for both insertion and search operations, showcasing the elegance of recursive algorithms in managing hierarchical data.

Input and Output Handling

The BST implementation allows users to input integers for populating the tree and specify a search value. Upon searching, the program outputs the number of iterations required to locate the desired value, thus providing insight into the efficiency of the search operation.

Asymptotic Analysis

The performance of the search operation in a BST is critically dependent on its height. In the worst-case scenario, where the tree becomes unbalanced, the time complexity can reach $O(n)$, where n represents the number of nodes. However, in a balanced BST, the height is logarithmic relative to the number of nodes ($O(\log n)$), ensuring more efficient operations.

Example Execution

Consider the following predefined values for populating the BST: {10, 5, 12, 3, 1, 13, 7, 2, 4, 14, 9, 8, 6, 11}. When searching for the value 9, the output might indicate that the search value was found in four iterations, illustrating the effectiveness of the BST structure.

Conclusion

The implementation of the Binary Search Tree efficiently manages data through organized insertion and search operations. Asymptotic analysis reinforces the importance of balanced structures for maintaining optimal performance. This foundational understanding of BSTs sets the stage for tackling more complex data structures and algorithms, ultimately enhancing software development practices.

Chapter 5

Exploring Non-Binary Trees

Introduction

In this chapter, I delve into my experiences and learnings regarding non-binary trees, particularly general trees, K-ary trees, and sequential trees. My main objective was to comprehend their structures, applications, and the underlying algorithms used for their implementation and traversal. This exploration involved practical exercises using the Jeliot environment, where I executed a Java algorithm designed for general trees. Through this process, I gained insights into the adaptability and complexity of these data structures.

Reactions and Discoveries

Working with non-binary trees was a journey filled with challenges and revelations. Unlike binary trees, which have strict structural limitations, non-binary trees offer a level of flexibility that mirrors real-world systems, such as file hierarchies and network architectures. This flexibility allowed me to appreciate the various applications of non-binary trees in everyday scenarios.

As I engaged with the algorithm and its implementation, I developed a deeper understanding of the complexities involved in tree traversal and node insertion. The process of navigating the tree illuminated the intricacies of these operations, distinguishing them from the more straightforward operations associated with binary trees.

Peer Feedback and Interactions

Throughout the unit, I received valuable feedback from my peers regarding the effectiveness of different tree traversal techniques and their implementations. These discussions were instrumental in broadening my perspective on tree structures and algorithms. The exchange of ideas fostered a collaborative learning environment, where we could explore the nuances of non-binary trees and the implications of various traversal methods on performance and efficiency.

Emotional Response

Initially, I found non-binary trees to be more complex than binary trees, which led to some feelings of overwhelm. However, as I progressed through the assignments and engaged in discussions, I began to feel more confident in my understanding of these structures. The hands-on experience of working with the Jeliot tool and analyzing tree algorithms provided a sense of accomplishment and a deeper appreciation for non-binary trees.

Key Learnings

Through this unit, I discovered several key concepts related to non-binary trees. One of the most significant insights was their adaptability compared to binary trees. I learned about unique tree structures such as K-ary trees and sequential trees, each with specific advantages and use cases. Additionally, I recognized the practical applications of these trees in everyday situations, such as organizing file systems and optimizing network routing.

Surprises and Challenges

One of the most fascinating aspects of this exploration was the adaptability of non-binary trees and how it affects traversal methods and overall performance. However, I encountered challenges in grasping the trade-offs between various tree structures, such as linked lists versus array-based implementations. Striking a balance between flexibility and operational efficiency proved to be a complex task, requiring careful consideration of the specific needs of the application.

Skills and Knowledge Gained

By the end of this unit, I had significantly improved my understanding of tree data structures, particularly in terms of their implementation, traversal, and asymptotic analysis. I feel more equipped to select the appropriate tree structure for various applications and to evaluate the efficiency of tree algorithms. This knowledge will undoubtedly serve as a foundation for further studies in data structures and algorithms.

Reflection on Learning Style

Through this experience, I realized that I excel in hands-on learning environments where practical demonstrations are utilized. The process of dissecting algorithms within the Jeliot environment solidified my understanding and made complex concepts more accessible. This realization will guide my future learning endeavors, as I seek opportunities for practical application and experimentation.

Application of Concepts

The concepts learned during this unit have broad applications in various fields of computer science. They can be utilized to enhance data storage and retrieval in file management systems or to develop efficient algorithms for network routing. Mastering these concepts prepares me for more advanced topics within data structures and algorithms, ultimately contributing to my growth as a computer scientist.

Conclusion

In summary, this chapter highlights the importance of balancing flexibility and efficiency in data structures, particularly in the context of non-binary trees. As I continue my studies, I will remain mindful of how different structures and algorithms impact performance, ensuring that I select solutions tailored to specific needs and constraints. The insights gained from this exploration will undoubtedly shape my future approach to data structures and algorithms.

Chapter 6

Understanding and Implementing Quicksort

Introduction

In this chapter, I will explore the quicksort algorithm, one of the most efficient and widely used sorting techniques in computer science. Quicksort exemplifies the divide-and-conquer approach, efficiently sorting data by partitioning arrays based on a chosen pivot. This chapter will discuss the algorithm's mechanics, its efficiency, practical implementation, and asymptotic analysis, drawing from recent assignments and discussions.

Overview of Quicksort

Quicksort operates by selecting a pivot element from an array and partitioning the other elements into two sub-arrays: those less than the pivot and those greater than it. The steps are as follows:

1. **Choose a Pivot**: The choice of pivot is crucial and can significantly impact performance.

2. **Partitioning**: Rearrange the array so that elements less than the pivot are on one side, and those greater are on the other.

3. **Recursive Sorting**: Recursively apply the same process to the left and right sub-arrays.

4. **Base Case**: The recursion stops when the size of the array is zero or one, indicating that the array is already sorted.

Implementation of Quicksort

The following Python implementation demonstrates the quicksort algorithm. It recursively sorts an array while tracking the number of exchanges made during the process.

```python
def quicksort(arr):
    if len(arr) <= 1:
        return arr
    else:
        pivot = arr[len(arr) // 2]
        left = [x for x in arr if x < pivot]
        middle = [x for x in arr if x == pivot]
        right = [x for x in arr if x > pivot]
        return quicksort(left) + middle + quicksort(right)

arr = [3, 6, 8, 10, 1, 2, 1]
print(quicksort(arr))
```

Java Implementation

In addition to the Python example, here is the Java implementation of quicksort, which includes a counter for the number of exchanges:

```java
public class QuickSortExample {
    static int exchangeCount = 0;

    public static void quickSort(int[] array, int low, int high) {
        if (low < high) {
            int pi = partition(array, low, high);
            quickSort(array, low, pi - 1);
            quickSort(array, pi + 1, high);
        }
    }
```

```java
public static int partition(int[] array, int low, int high) {
    int pivot = array[high];
    int i = low - 1;
    for (int j = low; j < high; j++) {
        if (array[j] < pivot) {
            i++;
            swap(array, i, j);
        }
    }
    swap(array, i + 1, high);
    return i + 1;
}

public static void swap(int[] array, int i, int j) {
    int temp = array[i];
    array[i] = array[j];
    array[j] = temp;
    exchangeCount++;
}

public static void main(String[] args) {
    int[] arr = {12, 9, 4, 99, 120, 1, 3, 10, 23, 45, 75, 69, 31, 88, 101, 14,
    System.out.println("Unsorted array:");
    for (int i : arr) {
        System.out.print(i + " ");
    }
    System.out.println();

    quickSort(arr, 0, arr.length - 1);

    System.out.println("Sorted array:");
    for (int i : arr) {
        System.out.print(i + " ");
    }
    System.out.println();
    System.out.println("Number of exchanges: " + exchangeCount);
  }
}
```

Asymptotic Analysis

Understanding the efficiency of quicksort is essential:

- **Best Case**: O(n log n) occurs when the pivot divides the array into two equal halves.
- **Average Case**: O(n log n) reflects the algorithm's performance in typical scenarios.
- **Worst Case**: O(n²) arises when the pivot consistently results in unbalanced partitions, such as always selecting the smallest or largest element.

Despite its worst-case scenario, quicksort is often faster than other O(n²) algorithms, such as insertion sort, due to its efficient average-case performance and lower constant factors.

Sorting Terminology

To understand quicksort better, it is essential to familiarize oneself with relevant sorting terminology:

- **Comparison Sorts**: Algorithms like quicksort that sort by comparing elements.

- **Exchange Sorts**: A subset of comparison sorts where elements are swapped (e.g., bubble sort, quicksort).

- **Divide and Conquer**: An approach used by quicksort and mergesort, where a problem is divided into smaller subproblems.

- **Stability**: A stable sort maintains the relative order of equal elements.

- **In-place**: An algorithm that sorts data without requiring additional storage.

Conclusion

Quicksort is a powerful and efficient sorting algorithm, well-suited for large datasets. Its implementation demonstrates the significance of the pivot selection and the partitioning process. Understanding quicksort's mechanics and analyzing its efficiency prepares me for tackling more complex sorting scenarios in computer science. The practical applications of this algorithm are vast, making it a fundamental tool in data processing operations.

Chapter 7

Buffer Pool Algorithms

In this chapter, we delve into the intricacies of buffer pool management through an exploration of three prominent page replacement algorithms: FIFO (First In, First Out), LRU (Least Recently Used), and LFU (Least Frequently Used). Each algorithm embodies distinct heuristics that dictate how pages are managed within a buffer, impacting system performance and efficiency. We will analyze each heuristic's operational principles, inefficiencies, and situational efficiencies, followed by a reflective account of my practical experiences with these algorithms through coding exercises.

7.1 FIFO (First In, First Out)

7.1.1 Heuristic Description

FIFO is a straightforward page replacement method grounded in the principle that the earliest page added to the buffer will be the first to be replaced when a new page is required. This approach functions akin to a queue; pages are appended at the back and removed from the front. The simplicity of this method makes it easy to implement and understand.

7.1.2 Inefficiency Conditions

Despite its simplicity, FIFO can be inefficient under certain conditions. A notable drawback arises when frequently accessed pages are evicted simply because they were loaded earlier. For instance, if a page with a value of 5 is accessed frequently but was initially loaded into the buffer first, it may be removed prematurely. This can lead to increased page faults, as the system must retrieve the page from secondary storage repeatedly.

7.1.3 Efficiency Situations

FIFO shines in scenarios where data is accessed in a sequential manner without frequent revisits to specific pages. For example, in applications like streaming services, where data is processed linearly, FIFO can efficiently manage buffer space without unnecessary disk reads.

7.2 LRU (Least Recently Used)

7.2.1 Heuristic Description

The LRU algorithm operates on the assumption that pages that have not been accessed for the longest duration are less likely to be needed in the near future. Consequently, it replaces the page that has not been used for the longest time, thus aiming to keep frequently accessed pages readily available.

7.2.2 Efficiency Conditions

LRU excels in environments where data access patterns exhibit temporal locality. In situations where users tend to revisit a small set of data before moving on, LRU effectively minimizes page faults by retaining the most relevant pages in the buffer. This characteristic makes it well-suited for applications where recent usage patterns can predict future needs.

7.3 LFU (Least Frequently Used)

7.3.1 Heuristic Description

LFU takes a different approach by tracking the frequency of access for each page. It evicts the page with the lowest access count, making it a candidate for replacement. This heuristic assumes that pages used infrequently are less likely to be required again.

7.3.2 Behavior in No Repeated Integers Scenario

In scenarios where all pages are accessed equally (e.g., no repeated integers), LFU operates similarly to FIFO. Each page is accessed once, leading to the eviction of the first loaded pages. However, this behavior reveals a limitation of LFU, emphasizing the importance of usage patterns in its effectiveness.

7.3.3 Repeated Values in Page Values

When certain pages are accessed more frequently than others, LFU demonstrates its strength by prioritizing retention of those frequently accessed pages. For instance, if the value 5 appears consistently, LFU reduces the likelihood of it being evicted, thereby minimizing subsequent page faults.

7.4 Practical Experience: Learning Journal

7.4.1 What I Did and How I Did It

This week, my primary focus was on implementing a buffer pool algorithm by exploring the heuristics of FIFO, LRU, and LFU. I began by familiarizing myself with the algorithm's structure through careful examination of the provided Java code. Using the Jeliot tool, I was able to visualize the algorithm in action. I tested various values, specifically running scenarios with two buffers and tracking how the buffer contents evolved over time.

7.4.2 Reactions to What I Did

Initially, I felt daunted by the complexity of the code and the nuances of each heuristic. However, as I continued to work through the exercises, my apprehension transformed into fascination. Observing how each heuristic managed the buffer pool in distinct ways provided valuable insights into their respective operational efficiencies and inefficiencies.

7.4.3 Feedback and Interactions

Engaging in discussions with my classmates further enriched my understanding. One peer suggested an alternative approach for LRU that utilized a stack-like structure to enhance tracking of recently used pages. Another classmate pointed out a potential issue with the LFU implementation regarding the proper resetting of the count array during page replacements. These interactions not only deepened my comprehension but also reinforced the collaborative nature of learning in this field.

7.4.4 Feelings and Attitudes

Throughout the week, I experienced a range of emotions, from initial frustration with the complexities of the task to a sense of achievement upon successfully running the algorithm. This journey underscored the importance of persistence and highlighted the joy that accompanies overcoming challenging problems.

7.4.5 What I Learned

My exploration into buffer management algorithms has significantly broadened my understanding of their practical applications. I analyzed the advantages and disadvantages of each heuristic, recognizing that while FIFO may offer simplicity, it can fall short in performance under certain conditions. In contrast, LRU and LFU present more sophisticated solutions, albeit with added complexity in monitoring usage patterns.

7.4.6 Surprises and Challenges

One of the most surprising aspects of my learning was witnessing how effectively the LFU heuristic performed with uneven access frequencies among pages. However, I also encountered challenges, particularly in maintaining accurate usage counts, especially when multiple pages had the same frequency. This experience highlighted the complexities of designing algorithms that efficiently handle diverse usage patterns.

7.4.7 Skills and Knowledge Gained

Through this week's exercises, I observed notable improvements in my Java programming skills, especially regarding array manipulation and data structures. Additionally, I gained a deeper understanding of the application of theoretical concepts in practical coding scenarios, enhancing my problem-solving capabilities.

7.4.8 Realizations as a Learner

I realized that hands-on practice and trial and error significantly enhance my comprehension of concepts. While theoretical study provides a solid foundation, actively engaging with algorithms through coding solidifies my understanding. This process has also reinforced the values of patience and perseverance in tackling challenging issues.

7.4.9 Application to Own Experience

The knowledge and skills acquired from this week's learning can be applied to real-world scenarios where efficient data management is critical. Understanding different heuristics empowers me to design systems that optimize resource management, whether in software development or IT infrastructure.

7.4.10 Important Reflection

A key takeaway from this week is the need to balance simplicity and efficiency in algorithm design. While straightforward algorithms like FIFO are easy to grasp, more intricate methods like LRU and LFU can yield superior performance in specific contexts. This insight encourages me to carefully consider these elements when developing systems and selecting appropriate algorithms.

Conclusion

This chapter has provided an in-depth exploration of buffer pool algorithms, highlighting the unique characteristics and operational principles of FIFO, LRU, and LFU. Through practical engagement with these heuristics, I have gained valuable insights into their real-world applications and the complexities inherent in algorithm design. The lessons learned this week will undoubtedly inform my ongoing development as a programmer and problem-solver, equipping me to tackle future challenges with confidence.

Chapter 8

Exploring Searching and Indexing

Algorithms

In this chapter, we will explore the significant concepts and applications of searching and indexing algorithms, focusing on their importance in computer science. We will discuss various algorithms, including Jump Search, Binary Search, Self-Organizing Lists, Hashing, and Tree-Based Indexing, as well as the Zipf distribution and its implications for data organization. This exploration is informed by both theoretical principles and practical implementations, culminating in a reflective assessment of the learning experience.

8.1 Introduction to Searching Algorithms

Searching algorithms are fundamental to data retrieval in computer science, enabling efficient access to information stored in various structures. Among the most commonly used searching algorithms are Jump Search and Binary Search, each with unique operational principles and efficiency characteristics.

8.1.1 Jump Search

Jump Search is an algorithm that reduces the number of comparisons needed to find a target value in a sorted array. By jumping ahead a fixed number of steps (the jump size) and then performing a linear search within the block where the target is likely located, Jump Search offers a balance between linear and binary search efficiencies. Its performance is particularly advantageous for large datasets, as it minimizes the number of comparisons required.

8.1.2 Binary Search

Binary Search operates on the principle of divide and conquer. It repeatedly divides a sorted array in half, eliminating half of the search space with each comparison. This logarithmic efficiency makes it an optimal choice for sorted datasets, significantly reducing search times compared to linear search methods.

8.2 Indexing Techniques

Indexing is a crucial aspect of data management that enhances retrieval speeds by organizing data in a manner that facilitates quick access. Hashing and Tree-Based Indexing are two prominent methods used to achieve this goal.

8.2.1 Hashing

Hashing transforms data into a fixed-size value (hash code), which serves as an index for storing records. This method enables direct access to data, drastically reducing search times. However, it also introduces the challenge of collision resolution, where multiple inputs generate the same hash code. Understanding the distinction between open and closed hashing, as well as various collision resolution techniques, is vital for effective implementation.

8.2.2 Tree-Based Indexing

Tree-Based Indexing, including structures like Binary Search Trees (BSTs) and B-Trees, organizes data hierarchically. This structure allows for efficient searching, insertion, and deletion operations. Tree-based indexes excel in maintaining sorted order and providing logarithmic access times, making them ideal for dynamic datasets.

8.3 The Zipf Distribution

The Zipf distribution is a noteworthy probability distribution observed in various datasets, where the frequency of an item decreases as its rank increases. Specifically, the item ranked first appears twice as frequently as the second, three times as frequently as the third, and so forth. This characteristic creates a situation where a small number of items are very common, while the majority are relatively rare.

8.3.1 Mathematical Representation

The Zipf distribution can be expressed mathematically as: $P(x) \propto x^{s1}$

Here, $P(x)$ represents the probability of the xth ranked item, and s is a parameter that influences the distribution's skewness. In many real-world contexts, s tends to hover around 1, signifying a pronounced drop-off in frequency as rank increases.

8.3.2 Applications in Natural Language Processing

A prime illustration of the Zipf distribution can be found in natural language processing (NLP). When analyzing word frequency in large corpora, common words such as "the" or "and" are frequently encountered. The frequency of these words diminishes significantly as we progress to less common terms. Understanding this distribution not only aids in effective data compression but also enhances our comprehension of linguistic structures.

8.4 Reflective Experience

8.4.1 Learning Journey

During this week in CS 3303, I immersed myself in the exploration of searching and indexing algorithms. Engaging with Clifford A. Shaffer's textbook, particularly Chapters 9 and 10, provided a solid theoretical foundation for my understanding. I took thorough notes on the various searching techniques and their practical implications.

Following my reading, I implemented several algorithms using Python, including Jump Search and Binary Search. This hands-on practice enabled me to observe firsthand the functionality and performance of these algorithms. Additionally, I experimented with hashing, testing both open and closed methods alongside collision resolution techniques.

8.4.2 Community Engagement

Participating in the discussion forum proved invaluable. I shared insights regarding the Zipf distribution and its applications, especially in NLP, a concept I initially found challenging. Through discussion, my understanding deepened as I connected theoretical principles to practical examples, such as word frequency analysis.

8.4.3 Feedback and Collaboration

Feedback from my peers and instructor was instrumental in refining my coding skills. One peer suggested improvements to the hash function I was developing, prompting me to revisit my code and enhance its efficiency. This collaborative exchange underscored the importance of peer feedback in the learning process, reinforcing the notion that collaboration fosters growth.

8.4.4 Emotional Journey

Initially, I felt overwhelmed by the array of new concepts presented. However, as I engaged more deeply with the material and began implementing the algorithms, my confidence grew. I realized that these algorithms were not merely theoretical constructs; they are practical tools essential for enhancing performance across various applications.

8.4.5 Insights Gained

Through my exploration, I gained a nuanced understanding of different search techniques and their significance in data retrieval. I learned about the performance trade-offs associated with various algorithms and how effective indexing can substantially improve search efficiency. The concept of the Zipf distribution expanded my perspective on data organization and retrieval, particularly in linguistic contexts.

8.4.6 Surprises and Challenges

I was particularly surprised by the efficacy of self-organizing lists, which dynamically rearrange themselves based on access frequency.

This feature sparked my curiosity about potential applications beyond standard lists, including dynamic databases and AI systems. Conversely, mastering collision resolution in hashing proved challenging. Striking a balance between efficient hash functions and effective collision resolution required careful consideration of theoretical and practical aspects.

8.4.7 Skills Development

Throughout this week, I honed my skills in analyzing and implementing algorithms, particularly in searching and indexing. The practical coding exercises not only improved my problem-solving capabilities but also deepened my appreciation for the significance of algorithmic efficiency in software development.

8.4.8 Self-Reflection as a Learner

I discovered that I learn best through a combination of theory and hands-on practice. While reading provides a foundation, applying concepts in code solidifies my understanding and reveals their real-world applications. Additionally, I recognized the value of connecting with peers for feedback, enhancing both my skills and comprehension.

8.4.9 Practical Applications

The insights gained this week are directly applicable to software development projects involving data retrieval. The knowledge of hashing and indexing will significantly enhance data storage and retrieval in upcoming initiatives, such as database management systems and search engines.

8.4.10 Future Considerations

A key takeaway from this week is the critical importance of algorithm efficiency in the ever-expanding field of data management. As data continues to grow exponentially, the need for rapid and efficient retrieval systems becomes increasingly vital. I am considering ways to implement these concepts to optimize performance in my current and future projects.

Conclusion

This chapter has provided an in-depth exploration of searching and indexing algorithms, highlighting their fundamental roles in data retrieval and management. The integration of theoretical knowledge with practical application has enriched my understanding of these concepts, emphasizing their significance in real-world contexts. The insights gained from the study of the Zipf distribution further enhance our comprehension of data organization and retrieval patterns, underscoring the interconnectedness of algorithm design and data behavior. This journey will undoubtedly inform my ongoing development as a programmer, equipping me to tackle future challenges with confidence and clarity.

Chapter 9

Recap and Summary

As we conclude this exploration of searching and indexing algorithms, it is essential to reflect on the key concepts, insights, and personal growth that emerged throughout this journey. This chapter will summarize the major topics covered, reinforce the significance of the material, and highlight the lessons learned in the context of both theoretical knowledge and practical application.

9.1 Overview of Key Concepts

Throughout this work, we delved into several fundamental algorithms that play critical roles in data retrieval and management:

1. **Searching Algorithms**: We examined key searching techniques, including:

    - **Jump Search**: A hybrid approach that reduces the number of comparisons by jumping ahead a fixed number of steps, striking a balance between linear and binary search efficiencies.
    - **Binary Search**: A highly efficient method that uses a divide-and-conquer strategy to minimize the search space, making it ideal for sorted datasets.

2. **Indexing Techniques**: Indexing serves as a foundation for efficient data retrieval:

- **Hashing**: This method allows for direct access to data through hash codes, although it presents challenges in collision resolution, which we explored through both open and closed hashing techniques.
- **Tree-Based Indexing**: Structures like Binary Search Trees (BSTs) and B-Trees organize data hierarchically, enabling logarithmic search times and efficient management of dynamic datasets.

3. **Zipf Distribution**: We discussed the Zipf distribution as a significant probability distribution found in various datasets, particularly in natural language processing. Understanding this distribution enhances our grasp of word frequency patterns and aids in data compression and retrieval.

9.2 Importance of Algorithmic Efficiency

A recurring theme throughout this exploration has been the critical importance of algorithmic efficiency in software development. As data continues to expand at an unprecedented rate, the need for rapid and effective data retrieval systems becomes essential. The insights gained regarding searching and indexing algorithms not only provide tools for optimizing performance but also emphasize the necessity of thoughtful design in software architecture.

9.3 Personal Growth and Learning

Reflecting on my personal journey, I recognized several significant areas of growth:

- **Hands-On Application**: Engaging in practical coding exercises allowed me to bridge the gap between theory and application, solidifying my understanding of algorithms through real-world implementation. The iterative process of coding, testing, and refining algorithms bolstered my confidence and problem-solving abilities.

- **Collaboration and Feedback**: Interacting with peers in discussion forums enriched my learning experience. The exchange of ideas and constructive feedback highlighted the value of collaboration in the learning process, demonstrating how different perspectives can deepen understanding and enhance skills.

- **Self-Discovery as a Learner**: I discovered that my learning style thrives on the integration of theory with practice. The combination of reading, implementing, and discussing concepts has proven to be an effective approach, allowing me to internalize knowledge and apply it meaningfully.

9.4 Future Applications

The principles and techniques explored throughout this work are directly applicable to various domains within software development. Understanding searching and indexing algorithms will enhance my capabilities in areas such as:

- **Database Management**: Efficient retrieval of data is paramount in database systems, where indexing and hashing play critical roles in performance optimization.

- **Natural Language Processing**: The insights gained from studying the Zipf distribution will inform my work in NLP, particularly in tasks related to text analysis, word frequency, and information retrieval.

- **Software Development Projects**: The knowledge of algorithmic efficiency and data management strategies will serve as a foundation for future projects, ensuring that I can create robust and efficient applications.

9.5 Conclusion

In summary, this exploration of searching and indexing algorithms has provided valuable insights into the principles and practices that underpin effective data retrieval. By combining theoretical understanding with practical application, I have developed a deeper appreciation for the significance of algorithmic efficiency and the impact it has on software development. As I move forward in my academic and professional journey, the lessons learned from this chapter will guide my approach to tackling complex data management challenges, empowering me to contribute effectively to the field of computer science.

Glossary

1. **Algorithm**: A step-by-step procedure or formula for solving a problem or completing a task.

2. **Buffer Pool**: A storage area in memory where data is temporarily held to improve the efficiency of data access.

3. **Data Structure**: A specialized format for organizing, processing, and storing data, enabling efficient access and modification.

4. **FIFO (First In, First Out)**: A page replacement algorithm where the oldest page in memory is replaced first.

5. **Hashing**: A process that transforms input data into a fixed-size string of characters, which typically appears random. It is used for fast data retrieval.

6. **Heuristic**: A problem-solving approach that employs a practical method not guaranteed to be perfect but sufficient for reaching an immediate goal.

7. **Jump Search**: A searching algorithm that divides a sorted array into blocks and performs a linear search within those blocks.

8. **LRU (Least Recently Used)**: A page replacement algorithm that replaces the least recently accessed page in memory.

9. **LFU (Least Frequently Used)**: A page replacement algorithm that removes the least frequently used page from memory.

10. **Natural Language Processing (NLP)**: A branch of artificial intelligence that deals with the interaction between computers and humans through natural language.

11. **Self-Organizing List**: A data structure that rearranges itself based on access frequency, optimizing search times.

12. **Tree-Based Indexing**: A method of organizing data in a hierarchical structure, allowing for efficient searching, insertion, and deletion operations.

13. **Zipf Distribution**: A probability distribution where the frequency of an item is inversely proportional to its rank in a frequency table.

Appendix

A. Code Snippets

A.1 FIFO Algorithm Implementation (Python)

```python
class FIFO:
    def __init__(self, capacity):
        self.capacity = capacity
        self.buffer = []

    def access(self, page):
        if page not in self.buffer:
            if len(self.buffer) >= self.capacity:
                self.buffer.pop(0)  # Remove the oldest page
            self.buffer.append(page)

# Example Usage
fifo = FIFO(3)
fifo.access(1)
fifo.access(2)
fifo.access(3)
fifo.access(4)  # This will evict page 1
print(fifo.buffer)  # Output: [2, 3, 4]
```

A.2 LRU Algorithm Implementation (Python)

```python
class LRU:
    def __init__(self, capacity):
        self.capacity = capacity
        self.buffer = {}

    def access(self, page):
        if page in self.buffer:
            self.buffer.pop(page)  # Remove and reinsert to update the order
        elif len(self.buffer) >= self.capacity:
            self.buffer.pop(next(iter(self.buffer)))  # Remove the least recently used page
        self.buffer[page] = None

# Example Usage
lru = LRU(3)
lru.access(1)
lru.access(2)
lru.access(3)
lru.access(2)  # Accessing page 2 again
```

B. Additional Readings

B.1 Recommended Textbooks

1. Shaffer, C. A. (2013). *A Practical Introduction to Data Structures and Algorithm Analysis (3rd ed.)*. Dover Publications.
2. Barnett, G., & Del Tongo, L. (2009). *Data Structures and Algorithms: An Annotated Reference with Examples*. Jones and Bartlett Publishers.

C. Useful Online Resources

1. GeeksforGeeks: A comprehensive resource for learning data structures and algorithms.
2. LeetCode: A platform for practicing coding problems and algorithm challenges.

D. Acknowledgments

I would like to thank my instructor and classmates for their valuable feedback and support throughout this course. Special thanks to the contributors of the resources and literature that greatly enhanced my understanding of data structures and algorithms.

Bibliography

Shaffer, C. (2011). *A Practical Introduction to Data Structures and Algorithm Analysis*. Virginia Tech. Retrieved from https://people.cs.vt.edu/shaffer/Book/JAVA3e20130328.pdf

Barnett, G., & Del Tongo, L. (2008). *Data Structures and Algorithms: Annotated Reference with Examples.* Dotnetslackers.

Shaffer, C. (2011). *A Practical Introduction to Data Structures and Algorithm Analysis.* Blacksburg: Virginia

Tech. Retrieved from https://people.cs.vt.edu/shaffer/Book/JAVA3e20130328.pdf

Algorithm animations and visualizations. (n.d.). Retrieved from http://www.algoanim.ide.sk/

Shaffer, C. (2013). A Practical Introduction to Data Structures and Algorithm Analysis. Prentice Hall. https://my.uopeople.edu/pluginfile.php/1861778/mod_page/content/4/Practical_Into_to_Data_Structures_and_Algorithms_-_Shaffer.pdf

Sorting algorithms animations. (n.d.). *toptal*. Retrieved from https://www.toptal.com/developers/sorting-algorithms

www.ingramcontent.com/pod-product-compliance
Lightning Source LLC
LaVergne TN
LVHW041612070526
838199LV00052B/3105